CRIME SCENE
INVESTIGATOR

TAMRA B. ORR

Published in the United States of America by Cherry Lake Publishing
Ann Arbor, Michigan
www.cherrylakepublishing.com

Content Adviser: law enforcement members
Reading Adviser: Marla Conn, ReadAbility, Inc.

Library of Congress Cataloging-in-Publication Data

Orr, Tamra.
  Crime scene investigator/Tamra Orr.
    pages cm.—(Cool STEAM careers)
  Includes index.
  ISBN 978-1-63362-556-3 (hardcover)—ISBN 978-1-63362-736-9 (pdf)—ISBN 978-1-63362-646-1 (pbk.)—
ISBN 978-1-63362-826-7 (ebook)
  1. Forensic sciences—Juvenile literature. 2. Criminal investigation—Juvenile literature.
  3. Crime scene searches—Juvenile literature. I. Title.

  HV8073.8.O762 2016
  363.25'2—dc23

          2015005357

Cherry Lake Publishing would like to acknowledge the work of
the Partnership for 21st Century Skills. Please visit www.p21.org
for more information.

Printed in the United States of America
Corporate Graphics

ABOUT THE AUTHOR

Tamra Orr is a full-time writer and author living in the gorgeous Pacific Northwest. She loves her job because she learns more about the world every single day and then turns that information into pop quizzes for her patient and tolerant adult children (ages 24, 21, and 18). She has written more than 400 nonfiction books for people of all ages, so she never runs out of material or fascination with the world around her.

TABLE OF CONTENTS

STEAM is the acronym for Science, Technology, Engineering, Arts, and Mathematics. In this book, you will read about how each of these study areas is connected to a career in crime scene investigation.

CHAPTER 1

INVESTIGATING A CRIME

Kira and her mother were watching television. The local news began, and the top story caught their attention.

"Today, the nation's 310th person was set free due to new **DNA** evidence," said the reporter. "After the man had been in prison for more than a decade, investigators proved that he did not commit the crime."

Kira looked at her mom. "How is that possible?" she asked. "Did the police make a mistake?"

Her mother shook her head. "When a person is accused of a crime, there are many people who work as

Many clues are too small to be seen without a microscope.

a team to gather evidence. It sounds like one crime scene investigator missed something—or another one just discovered new clues."

Being a crime scene investigator (CSI) is a complex, fascinating, and important job that affects the lives of countless people. It means finding clues to crimes, from **homicides** and assaults to armed robberies, home invasions, and burglaries. The news often features these crimes on television. A crime has been committed. Yellow tape is put up to keep

Dusting for fingerprints can be one of the most important steps in an investigation.

spectators from entering the area. People with specialized tool kits arrive in official vehicles. Everyone gets out of the way to let the crime scene investigators begin their search for evidence!

Once on the scene, these special investigators are responsible for interviewing witnesses and examining, photographing, sketching, and processing any clues they find. Often they work as a team with a leader, photographer, sketcher, and evidence recorder. Each person has a special role. Leaders assign duties and make sure the scene is secure so evidence cannot be **contaminated**. Photographers take pictures of everything in the area. Sketchers draw detailed pictures of people involved in the crime. Evidence recorders describe every clue they find in a special **log**, or journal.

In some situations, additional specialists may be called. A bomb technician is brought in if there is any kind of explosive at the scene. In a suspicious death, **entomologists** may be asked to study bugs

THINK ABOUT SCIENCE

The science behind crime scene detection is always changing and improving. Fingerprints on items like guns and bullets have long been clues to follow in a crime. Now, a new technique is making it easier to find important details. A process in England applies an electrical charge to bullet casings. This charge makes it possible to detect if sweat from fingers has affected the metal. If so, fingerprints can be discovered on a bullet after it has been fired and even if they're wiped off!

By looking at bugs found on a dead body, a CSI can sometimes estimate how long ago the person died.

[21ST CENTURY SKILLS LIBRARY]

that are present on a body to help estimate how long that person has been dead.

No matter what kind of responsibility a specific CSI has, it involves a lot of paperwork. Every crime requires a worksheet with clear, detailed descriptions of what happened, a photo log of every picture taken, multiple sketches and diagrams for reference, and evidence record logs that list every clue. All of these details will be needed later when the **forensic** department begins piecing the crime together. CSIs must be **meticulous** about paperwork so their results will stand up to challenges in court.

CHAPTER 2

SEARCHING FOR CLUES

Some evidence at a crime scene is huge. You wouldn't miss a crushed car or a burned building, but what about a muddy footprint or a torn fingernail? How easily could a mysterious fiber or strand of hair be overlooked? Once discovered, each piece of evidence needs to be analyzed. Every piece of evidence can provide essential clues.

The first steps of any investigation are almost always the same. First, the CSI must determine the extent of the crime. Is there a single victim or multiple victims? Do clues stay within the building or lead around the block?

How much of the area should be secured so that evidence doesn't become lost or damaged?

Next, the CSI does a walk-through of the crime scene, noting the most important details. Finally, the CSI calls in any necessary experts and requests additional equipment.

Not every car accident is really an accident. Sometimes CSIs need to investigate.

Every piece of evidence needs to be labeled.

In a murder investigation, the CSI will look for possible clues before the body is moved or touched. Are there any marks or stains on the clothing? Are there obvious injuries to the body? Is there blood? If so, the pattern of the blood spatter often holds details about what actually happened. While the majority of blood is usually from the victim, some might also be from the suspect, and if so, it can help pinpoint identity. Other bodily fluids, including saliva and vomit, contain essential information as well.

Investigators often search a crime scene in a pattern to ensure it is thoroughly covered. They may choose an inward spiral, starting at the outside of the scene and working inward. They can also start at the center and work out. Another option is the grid pattern, where investigators walk in parallel lines from one side of the scene to the other. Or they may use the zone method, where each investigator is assigned a specific section to examine.

Crime scene tape requests that people who aren't investigators avoid the area.

Looking for clues may sound simple, but the CSI needs to pay attention to every detail. A lot of evidence is tiny and requires patience and a keen eye to find. CSIs often search for a single strand of hair, fiber, or thread. They may hunt for tiny pieces of glass, paint chips, or soil samples. All possible pieces of evidence are placed in specific evidence bags. Labels are carefully filled out with the date, time, and location of where the bag's contents were found so that nothing important is forgotten or left out. In addition to plastic and paper bags, CSIs also use airtight metal cans to hold larger pieces of evidence. Each piece is put into a separate container. Mishandled evidence can ruin even the strongest cases, so CSIs know that following **protocol** is the number one priority with every single clue.

THINK ABOUT TECHNOLOGY

*In 1776, Paul Revere identified the body of a general based on a false tooth that Revere had made for him from a walrus tusk. Identifying a person has come a long way since then. Recently, a California police department has been testing a state-of-the-art handheld gadget called the Mobile Biometric Device. It can scan fingerprints, **irises**, and other biological information on the scene, and then communicate the information to remote international databases. This makes it possible to identify suspects and victims immediately.*

CHAPTER 3

BRINGING IN THE EQUIPMENT

In small police departments, a single CSI might be expected to play many roles. Each role requires different equipment.

Fingerprint experts use different brushes and powders along with tape, lift cards, and a magnifying glass to preserve prints for analysis. They look for prints on clothing, doors, furniture, and other surfaces. "Fingerprints" can also come from hands, toes, and feet. **Latent** fingerprints are the most common to find at a scene. They are caused when dirt, sweat, or other residue

Fingerprint experts can help identify a suspect or victim.

is pushed onto another object. They can be left on objects such as mirrors, glass, paper, and clothing. When these prints are checked against a national database called the Integrated Automated Fingerprint Identification System (IAFIS), it can help lead authorities right to the suspect.

Crime scene photographers typically bring several cameras to the scene. They also carry extra batteries, lenses, filters, and a tripod. Their skills must be top-notch, because unlike subjects in most types of

*Crime scene photographers make sure to document
every possible piece of evidence.*

[21ST CENTURY SKILLS LIBRARY]

CSIs use special equipment to make sure that nothing tiny gets missed.

professional photography, these subjects can't be moved and the lighting can't be changed. Photos are taken of the surrounding rooms or neighborhood, as well as of clues, vehicles, and other related evidence—not just the victims. These photographers are CSIs who take accurate and detailed pictures to be used as part of court cases, forensic reports, and for analysis and measurement.

Investigators who collect blood samples carry **sterile** cloth, glass microscope slides, distilled water, scalpels, tweezers, and scissors. Other investigators specialize in

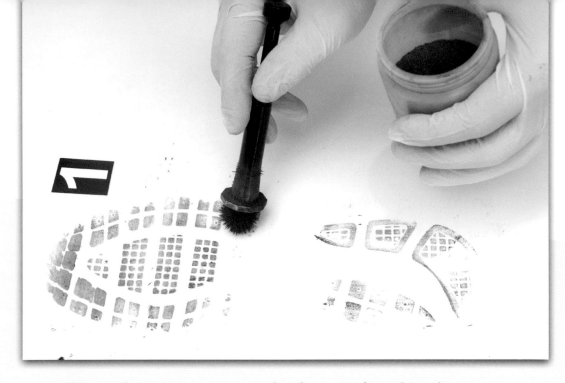

Looking at shoe prints, a CSI can often figure out facts about the wearer.

making casts of footprints. They carry a special powder to mix with water. These investigators may also make casts of tire tracks from the vehicles that have been in the area. A shoe print can help determine a shoe size, whether the shoe is for a woman or man, or even what brand it is.

Most investigators have a standard set of equipment they carry, including a flashlight, a clipboard for paperwork, pens, a compass, chalk, and police tape. Sometimes they use hammers, screwdrivers, wrenches, shovels, and wire cutters, too. Special investigators who are called to crime scenes that may have a **biohazard** wear sterile suits and disposable gloves, booties, face masks, and aprons.

Having the right equipment for the right job is key to being successful. CSIs focus on making sure they arrive at the scene with everything they need to help find their clues.

THINK ABOUT ENGINEERING

What do engineers have to do with blood spatter? Daniel Attinger is an engineer studying the shape and size of stains based on a method of pattern recognition. He and his team are studying the way blood droplets splash, splatter, and evaporate. He hopes to develop a 3-D measurement device to use at crime scenes. "I always want to show people how important engineering is to help people with their lives and with society," Attinger says. "I think engineers can do a lot to make the world a better place."

Looking to the Future

What might happen in the future to change crime scene investigation? Will it look anything like the science-fiction novels with robots fighting battles instead of humans? Or police officers being able to stop crimes before they happen?

In some ways, the future is already here. Robots are being used to handle potentially explosive devices. One day robots may be used for finding armed suspects without risking the lives of police officers or others. Computers have already sped up the search process for

Robots like this one can handle dangerous materials so that the human investigators don't need to.

many police departments. Computers can connect distant investigators to one another and to international evidence databases. Technical advances allow crime scene investigators to uncover more and more evidence. However, it's the people behind the instruments and equipment who are responsible for accuracy. They are accountable for handling even the smallest bit of evidence correctly.

What devices are in the works that will change the job of the CSI? Already a number of high-security

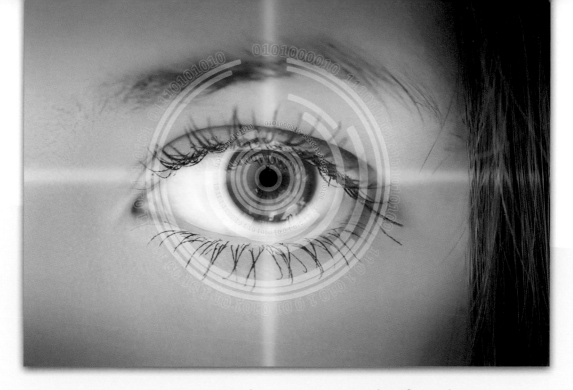

Iris scanning is one way that computers can identify people.

companies are using programs that scan the iris of the eye for positive identification. Fingerprint readers that electronically scan fingerprint patterns and **digitize** them are being used more often. Some experts even believe that a specific type of odor detector will someday be used to track a suspect like a bloodhound can.

Also assisting CSIs is the growing use of security cameras. These are becoming common outside businesses, in subway stations, and in apartment lobbies. If a crime is committed on a street, investigators will review videos from businesses nearby to see if they can identify a suspect. However, some people object to the use of these cameras, believing that their right to privacy is being violated. The laws addressing this differ among states.

THINK ABOUT ART

Documenting a crime scene depends on many people, especially the CSI who focuses on sketching the scene. This CSI carries graph paper, pens and pencils, measuring tapes, rulers, and a notepad and uses them to sketch everything from the position of a victim to the precise location and relationship of objects and evidence at the scene. These drawings become a permanent part of the record and are often used in court. Rough sketches are developed on scene and not done to scale. Final sketches are done in ink or on a computer, and depict all relevant items of evidence.

CHAPTER 5

BECOMING A CSI

There is a reason that TV shows such as *CSI* and its spin-offs are so popular. Many people are fascinated by mysterious crime scenes. Real-life CSIs are the heroes in these stories, both on screen and off. Their dedication, time, skills, and education help to take the questions out of the crime and provide the solutions instead.

If you want to pursue a career as a CSI, high school science and math classes are important. Chances are, you will need these if you pursue a college degree. In addition, it is important to develop your critical thinking and

A background in chemistry could be useful for a CSI.

problem-solving skills. You should also have the ability to pay attention to detail and to communicate well, both in writing and speaking. Each one of these qualities will be called on in the field of crime scene analysis.

Most CSIs have a bachelor's degree in criminal justice or forensic science, although a few smaller law enforcement agencies will accept a student with only a GED. Some departments may also require you to complete police academy training, as some CSIs are police officers first.

A CSI needs to be careful to not disturb the crime scene before it has been photographed.

In addition to the four-year college degree, some CSIs go on to earn specific licenses and certification. They may do so in order to apply for specific jobs, to follow personal passions and interests, or in hopes of earning higher salaries. Some of the choices include training in **arson**, courtroom **testimony**, footwear and tire tread identification, blood pattern analysis, and evidence photography.

According to the Bureau of Labor Statistics, the median pay for a CSI is $52,840 a year, or roughly

[21ST CENTURY SKILLS LIBRARY]

$25.41 an hour. A median salary is defined as the amount that half the workers earn more than and half earn less than across the country. The majority of CSIs work in police departments and offices, although some work in crime labs, **morgues**, and medical examiners' or **coroners**' offices.

If you like solving mysteries, finding clues, and helping to determine someone's guilt or innocence, a career as a crime scene investigator might be the perfect choice. Having a strong stomach doesn't hurt either!

THINK ABOUT MATHEMATICS

Crime scene investigating has a great deal to do with math, because a lot of clues depend on their measurements. So doing well in math classes is a great first step to this career. For example, CSIs need to be able to calculate the length of a person's gait or the weight and height of a suspect based on the depth of a footprint. Others use equations of time and distance to create a radius in which a suspect could have traveled since committing a crime. Math is also used to determine pathways of falling objects such as bullets or blood.

THINK ABOUT IT

More and more public places are using security cameras. Some people think that this lowers the amount of crime in those places, but other people think it is a violation of privacy. What do you think? Are there any security cameras where you live? Find out what the laws are in your state. Would you make them tougher? Why or why not?

Working as a crime scene investigator can turn into an extremely emotional job. A CSI doesn't know what he or she will find when arriving at a crime scene. After a particularly tragic case, a CSI may need to go to counseling to deal with the violent things that he or she saw. How do you think CSIs are trained for dealing with the violence in their jobs? How do you think that counseling can help?

LEARN MORE

FURTHER READING

Bertino, Anthony J. *Forensic Science: Fundamentals and Investigations.* Mason, OH: Cengage Learning, 2008.

Miller, Connie C. *Crime Scene Investigators: Uncovering the Truth.* North Mankato, MN: Capstone Press, 2008.

Mooney, Carla. *Forensics: Uncover the Science and Technology of Crime Scene Investigation.* White River Junction, VT: Nomad Press, 2013.

Murray, Elizabeth. *Forensic Identification: Putting a Name and Face on Death.* Minneapolis: Twenty-First Century Books, 2012.

Young, Karen Romano. *Science Fair Winners: Crime Scene Science.* Washington, DC: National Geographic, 2009.

WEB SITES

A2Z Home's Cool: Crime Scene Investigation for Kids
http://a2zhomeschooling.com/explore/chemistry_kids/csi_unit_study
_forensics_for_kids
Try solving some of these imaginary crimes using tips in these articles.

Kids Ahead: Crime Scene Investigation Activities
http://kidsahead.com/subjects/10-crime-scene-investigation/activities
Try some of these activities to see what it's like to be a crime scene investigator.

GLOSSARY

arson (AHR-suhn) the crime of setting fire to property with the intention of destroying it

biohazard (BYE-oh-haz-urd) a biological agent that constitutes a threat to humans

contaminated (kuhn-TAM-uh-nay-tid) impure or unsuitable through contact with something else

coroners (KOR-uh-nurz) officials who investigate sudden, violent, or unnatural deaths

digitize (DIJ-i-tize) convert to digital form for use on a computer

DNA (DEE EN AY) deoxyribonucleic acid, a main component of genetics

entomologists (en-tuh-MOL-uh-jists) scientists who study bugs and insects

forensic (for-EN-sik) using science and technology to investigate evidence and establish facts for use in court

homicides (HAH-mi-sidez) murders

irises (EYE-ris-iz) the colored portions of eyes

latent (LAY-tuhnt) present but not readily visible or evident

log (LAWG) journal or reporting book

meticulous (muh-TIK-yuh-luhs) very careful and thorough; paying great attention to detail

morgues (MORGZ) places where bodies of dead people are kept until they are released for burial

protocol (PROH-tuh-kawl) the correct rules for the way something should be done

sterile (STER-uhl) free from germs and dirt

testimony (TES-tuh-moh-nee) a formal statement given by a witness or an expert in a court of law

INDEX